VIGNETTE

VIGNETTE

Solaia Suherman

Books That Matter

VIGNETTE

Copyright © 2023, Solaia Suherman

Published by:
Books That Matter
an imprint of Blooming Twig
New York / Oklahoma

All rights reserved.

No part of this publication may be reproduced, stored in a retrieval system, stored in a database and/or published in any form or by any means, electronic, mechanical, photocopying, recording or otherwise, without the prior written permission of the publisher.

Paperback ISBN 978-1-61343-135-1

To the faces, places that inspired it.

TIME

Affogato

contact, metal, cream, tongue,
melt, it melts at the touch
of my tongue.
bittersweet,
the flavours disperse
musical notes,
spreads like mycelium on a canvas
a smear of fresh oil paints,
affogato   it's what it is,
the dessert that cures melancholia
sweet like golden hour,
a playground, the treble chatter
of children riding up and
down a breeze
round in embrace,
but bitter,
but serious,
but the thought of dinner,

the thought of growing up,
and growing old,
and growing dull.
taste, don't swallow,
it's just a dessert,
vision fades,
it's just a dessert,
but I can't not remember.

Chronicle

i awake to the sound of noise;
chatter, plates on plates,
echoing off aged white walls &
night-stained wood,
pull the curtains in two,
check the time. 9:06.

burning butter wraps
the kitchen air,
& i scrape away the black
from the bread. 10:12.

what if i hadn't
checked the time?

In a Minute

it's 6:27pm.
        laughs ride up the building's body:
        vines — downstairs, a dinner party,
        where silverware chimes in breeze.
a mother's child strides towards its shadow
cast on grass still dewed with rain, its shadow
stretched a couple years older, men that have
weathered with age, elongated, a couple years younger.
        it's 6:28pm. they're still complaining about
        cramps.
        the balcony. the evening mesh. my tea is cold.
it's 6:29pm. the laughs, shadows, cramps, tea
have gone away.

Timeline

and in the next second —

                we're in another moment.

    we follow this line of time, as if
    we didn't know, any better
    we let ourselves walk blindly

perhaps, losing
our voice, shouting
at   future's cloud, that
                                  howls,

    yet, we keep following

                                perhaps, losing
                                our limbs, crawling
                                into

past's burrow, that
wails,

yet, we keep walking

beckoning our bodies to fall
& spring, to be tossed
& turned by
tsunami
after tsunami

we fight
for the surface

another second,
to breathe.

Artichoke Heart

don't choke on this heart.

as i rode in the rain,
wind cut my eyes.
to my left,

a couple, they wore snow hair
hands weathered with age,
wheelchairs as thrones &
tanks of air to breathe,
to live, to see

a sunset —

what if
this was the last sunset
they saw?
then, they saw it together.

they stared on,

at the empty
bowl of the setting sun.

Venetian Finish

remember my face in the ripples of sun
                     & the shadow of my smile
cast flat against the walls, naked walls
where imagination breaks itself,
blank walls, unbearably empty walls
walls you see in your mind's eye
now, that we mark with metal,
now, forever to stay,
                   use them as floors.

Honesty, the best policy

my tongue's not acid, but
velvet and vertigo and unsaid
words that bind us how ribs
bind air.

my tongue's
a knot of
secrets,
that i'll tell you
one day.

Freeze-Frame

that moment will never return,
no, that moment will soon lose itself
in the fabric of time
in a matter of,
now.

just now, i wandered the streets with
a camera in pursuit of preserving a
moment, in time
who's transience will soon act upon
itself, but the frustration,
of seeing a perfect moment,
only to be a moment too late at the snap
of the lens,
and as the evening wore thin,
i wore tired
of grasping tableaus
in movement

and decided,
to just let the moment,
be a moment,
a flicker in time, a grain
of dust, a ghost,

no one has the power to make something transient,
transcend.

Burning

for a moment,
i thought the building
was on fire.
from a distance,
time slows;
an unreal reflection on its face
it seemed to glow,
radiantly, pulse,
but, it was just the sun,
and the evening moved on,
with the last flood of midas silk,
the building blazed on.

Glitch

one day,
i too will be a
poor,
fallen leaf.
i'll fall behind, give up treading against the current,
catching the horizon
collecting the ocean;
i'll begin turning into a blur,
a glitch in the system,
left behind in the
string of time,
as the world lives on
without,
i'll make my past my present
and grow old, and tired,
and forgotten;
and I'll sink in my frail bones,
and I'll give in to the flow of the stream,

and let the river, take me
because now,
now, all I have is the river.

Age

carve within me: the crow's feet,
        staple into me: the smile lines,
                give me proof: that i have lived.

if only we could press 'pause'

I.

Suppose it all
stopped.

> the dog is in the air,
> the house of cards leans,
> sunlight's no longer fluid,
> no noise left to hear,
> not even static
> no, breath left to breathe,

II.

If the world stopped,
I would run across

crossroads,
to meet the sea
where gulls hover over blue,
I'll dip myself in the waveless,
currentless bowl
& try to find an answer
to it all

                but fail, because
                I'm scouring the ends
                of the earth to
                find an answer
                in a narrative.

III.

What I'll find is a bouquet
of roses, though
ashen,
eyes, salt-seared,

world, sparkling,
beckoning,
saying:
come closer.

& I'll come to understand that
they're not roses,
but a bouquet of gunpowder,
sitting on the wind.

Wait

there are seeds within me
that wait for the
world to water
them, and i did
wait, for long enough,
only to find the
world, waiting
at my feet.

When will it come?

under the glow
of the tropic sun
sat and thought
for a lot
and by dusk —
nothing.

Algorithmic Memoir

Turn the page,

        I thought I saw an eagle,
        but it was just a kite.

'Chapter 16,'
        It's time to pack up my
        memories,
        but how can I,
        when I had the same
        person on my mind,
        a year ago today,

They're walking back,
        and I'm in a bind,

Turn the page,

        I saw an eagle.

'Chapter 16,'

        I woke up with a
        fly in my eye,
        How do I write on?

*Loving you drains all
the love from me,*

Now, I've set you aside,

        *But I still wish you had remembered
what day it is today.*

Again

My head can't wrap itself around the fact
that it's been a year,

March glares at me now,
March, again,
pierces through my skin
like I'm transparent,
asking why I'm still here, in the same place.

Last March felt
two dreams (and a nightmare) ago,
crisp, cold-cut, candid March
asks why I'm still in the box
I made,
why I'm still buried in dirt
I created.

A March ago,

I was on a trapeze.
This March,
I still am.

01/01

Is it déjà vu?
I slept through the countdown,
yet the turn of the new year still happened
in the thick of my dreams.
I woke up expecting to feel reformed,
as if I had somehow put last year's me to bed
and by some magical spell, begun again as a blank canvas.
But, as my eyes adjusted to this tomorrow,
everything from yesterday seemed to have stayed,
the canvas, a painting

TOUCH

Touch

i want to touch things
and feel things touch me back,
even when i reach out to grasp the grains
of 6-o'clock light,
i want to feel it on my skin,
i want to feel it all — the kind of warmth that melts you,

the feeling of falling sand,
each grain, other to
each grain, apart,

i want to touch,
i want touch,

yet, all i feel is nothing,
nothing touching me back.

Ace

every morning unfurls itself
to habit, pattern, ritual,

                      midnight water runs
                      from tap, showerhead,

walking on the sliver
of day & night,
the window, outside,
outside the sky whispers
in pink,

                      clothe myself in sheets of
                      paper &
                      lacklustre loafers,

        out
        the
        firm
        door.

every morning, we drive
like freedom,
while my eyes adjust
to this new reality,
letting remnants of
last night's dream
suspend,

                                      every morning, concrete
                                      glides past us,
                                      we talk

until we reach the harbour,
speed away from
dawn, into blue.
docks, ships, cargo,

                & we drive,
                past a great, big ship
                of the same sort, in the
                same place, every morning,

      always,
       ever-present,
        firmer than a memory

& every morning,
written on its face
something new:

  'Brilliant Ace'   'Miraculous Ace' 'Gracious
        Ace'

   every morning,
   we read,

    let it
    touch us,
      & then, we don't feel so

      untouched,

> so unknown,
> so unrecognisable —

'You have reached your destination.'

Numb

then, i lost myself like a lamb, and watched, as if breathing.
i tried nibbling my numbness away. it stayed, and ate me
inside out.
what's this? i pulled a string from my spine: a nerve.
suppose i still felt,
a bruise? a cut? still, too much,
they say, torn flesh grows gems;
something spilled from my stomach.
i'm not hollow, i promise,
but when i heard the arrow shoot through space,
it stopped before I felt the
pang.

The Space Between Us

i'm trying to remember what it felt like to feel

gazing into your seafoam gaze

fleeting,

yet ripe,
ripe, ripe —
nectar on the tongue

in your breath i've memorised

the ear's cave
knee's peak,

paper mache skin,

i hold our silence like glass,

i eat your words like ruins,
and clasp the space between our worlds.

do you know me?

I made eye contact with narcissus.

it is almost as if
i can't look into another
eye and not see
myself

~

dipping into the
pond you
hovered upon
so still,
you sank into your
own reflection,
warped perceptions
for the sake of
love,
& drowning,

~

if you look at me,
who do i see?

hands

hold hands

                    hold glass, tucked

away, between the

                    gap in the legs, hold

time, hold hair, hold

                    fruits of labour,

the crack between

                    worlds, hands hold

hope, hold you

                        hold on,

a hold

            on none.

Ritual

i dip my finger into a
cup of wood-red tea
to remind myself of
its burnt-umber softness
that cures me of
bitterness.

Constellation of Flesh

your body is not a house
you can
break, then repair,
shatter,
then rearrange,
your pelvis can't hold up a torso of
midnight awake-ness
anymore,
neither can the lungs gather the grace
that rains,
nor cup
in
its
branches
the
things beyond

Walking

a day of walking, walking, walking
to nowhere,
walking aimlessly,
walking absent from
destination,
brushing past the sleeves, shoulders, scents,
skins of somebodies,
at least, to me,
i'm a ghost, in this sun drenched city,
the sun echoes on my skin — for it glares at me —
the afternoon,
the humid, humid air,
the concrete pavements
and the odd, claustrophobic openness
of the streets
and the artificial notes of fresh-cut rose leaves,
and above all, the breaths, the tears, and dew
of a thousand strangers.

i love this city
the way i love the ocean
like the ocean, the city flows through me,
as i follow, flow, from person, to person,
riding the rhythm
the current of this crowd

We're Not Really Strangers

no matter how lost,
how deserted
you are,
the world unfurls itself
to a million acts
that touch.

'it doesn't come at a cost'
says a stranger,
'don't worry'
as i wandered the ghost streets of the city
moon high and hazed
they sent me to familiarity,
to life,
human, to human —
it's beautiful, really
that goodness still exists
in this wild purgatory.

tonight,
i'll sleep in peace,
because that stranger taught me
that no matter the context of you,
you'll be guided home

The Grab Driver

'see you' spilled
  from my teeth,
though we knew
  we would never
see each other
  again,
or, if fate allows,
  when we do
we would slip
  in & out of
periphery
  & sliding doors
almost as if
  we were strangers.

Interactions

These little interactions
with strange, new skins,
meeting, face-to-face, with another somebody,
These special, little interactions
where you open up your mind and heart
to listen, and to speak
words, in creation — we bounce off and absorb one another,

These are precious interactions
because all of a sudden, someone else is a part of your world,
and you, a part of theirs.
But, sooner or later, their faces, voices, names will
slip away from your memory —
they will, again, turn into strangers,
and dust.

Connection

    we had time — at least, enough to hold,
    i remember smelling a storm on its path,
    but we've cancelled our plans,

the skies, a glass dome, bit into my skin,
and all i saw was movement
a great arc of swirling grey
whispers of azure that opened and closed,
like gateways into
purity.
there's so much world.
    — *so, this is what flying feels like,*

i remember when you breezed through my
hair, and traced
my face, don't forget.
    — *so, this is what loving feels like,*

maybe it was the rain,
but it poured from my eye's vessel
dripping, new,
we moved in lost languages.
      — so, this is understanding,

no, it really was the rain,
slowly, gently, bead,
by bead,
pearl,
by pearl,
the forest
hushed a communal hush.
we fluttered our eyes
shut.
we breathed in our
mother's breath.
we let the rain,
rain.
      — so, this is connection.

MRT

in, out, in, out,
the rhythm of the city
sliding doors,
in, out,
people, people of all
a gathering in this tube
this loophole in time,
yet anonymous
each their own worlds
each head down,
isolated, lost in thoughts, blocking out
the world, covered in sound,

in this wormhole,
controlled chaos,
sitting without a purpose
but walking with a mission,
in, out, in, out,

of your life,
in, out, in, out,
weaving through fragments of
nobodies,
memories, masks, inertia, space,
in, in, in, in,
falling into
yourself.

Admiration

the people I admire most
are the ones who don't fear
having their head
in the clouds,
all the while staying grounded
on this earth
of unseen realities.

Popo

she reminds me of home.
dew on her face
hope hasn't left her with age
the valley between her brows
how her eyes bow,
the mark by her lip
bloomed wisdom,
soft strength
ordained upon her head,
roots bleached with time,

she kisses cheeks like
fireworks on the 4th,
and smells of tiger balm,

ylang-ylang

jasmine

rosewater

eucalyptus.

Dominos

so, that's how the
pieces fell —
                    into place,

for this moment
to bud,
in our narrative.

Shower Head

Under running water
I let my mind wander
into cracks and crevices
and let it roam
beyond the glass box I'm in,
in the steam, I breathe my own thoughts
before something new unwraps itself before me
and I come running out of the mist,
dripping with inspiration.

Realness

because all there was left to feel
was realness,
so real it wasn't real anymore —
surreal,
hyper-real,
so real it came, and went,
as a dream.

this is flesh, though,
flesh on flesh,
though, our eyes found each other's,
we're still finding reality,
though we breathe,
we're still searching for air.
all i found left to do
was shake my head
in protest against
this vivid, moving

moment,
being reality.

since we parted,
the dream went on.

Story of a Moth and Flame

and i press you into my mind,
like sweet sixteen flowers pressed between pages
to blow out candles is to blow out an end,
a start has come,
marked by the scent you left on my sweater:
smokescreen, city lights, cabin,
your presence, a cradle,
as i walked through the world of signs, symbols
you were there, though
unseen,
presence, a gust,

i am the moth to the flame,
the moth rolls out my neck
the moth trickles down my tongue
the moth escapes my mouth,
fur to flame,
breathless,

i gasp for more air
air, more air
more your air.

the roof, the full moon,
the ladies', the garden,
only then is the scent a person,
only then is the moth ashen.

you wrote,
i spoke,

as i walk through a world of faces, places,
i hold onto your scent that now
twists with sun and sweat
bleeds into my own skin
perhaps i'm yours —
and i burn you into my mind once again,
before sleep steals night
comes dream.

Mangosteen

and i cracked open the stone
that broke with tyrian purple
indigo rain, magenta
husk — crush,
something pure is swelling
inside: fruit like flesh,
snow skin, bone skin,
perfectly ripe.

TRAVERSE

December Monday

It's been windy,
And everything seems a little clearer
Combs my hair like a mother
Embraces my world,
The sky's at my feet
And I see the stark silhouette

Of a bird fly by
Above, below
Taped to the grey-blue sphere
Silently riding the tides of air.

Does this wind mark a new beginning?
I can taste the equinox
Salt air
The world races on

But I took the lark's feather
To lose, to win.

Dive

I.

the soul wants to

plunge into

the depths of

the skies,

spread itself across

the moving colours,

inhale all the

grey,

the kingdoms

of dew,

dive into

the great expanse,

of the

heart.

II.

she dove

upwards,
as if impossibility
in the flesh.
was it even flesh?

III.
with pencil, i wrote on
the building's body,
and somehow felt
in control of
it all.

The Potter

what if it was me who
wrote this story?
      did i forge my dream in
      gold & carve
      it into earth?
did i hammer it till
the sun met its
sphere,
      or mould it like
      clay —
when i awoke from
reaching the ends of
my hair,
and back,
      i understood,
      that i was the potter.

Thought

and it provokes me
that my thoughts lean not on a string,
but on a stream.
winding — never straight.
stars like dust
in the firmament of
my mind.
'i must not get distracted' —
yet,
i drift down the infinite, winding stream:
following

Travelling

I don't think I can tell
fact from fiction.
I fell asleep in the sky
and woke up in some foreign land,
then, like a dream, roamed its
unfamiliar alleyways, streets, crossroads
that all wove into a web of places
language, too, felt like wind,
currency, like water.

My phone died,

and I feel like a knot
has been unknotted,
my eyes feel a little wider —
like an unveiling to the world;

I've never felt such a strong desire
for presence, to let the crowd take me,
to find, to listen to impulse,
in that moment.

Now, I have nowhere to hide behind,
and all I see are the millions of possibilities
this world opens itself up to.

All there is to do, is to exist
in this vibrant, breathing place
that I now tread upon
in another way.

Observations in the City at Night

In my sweaty, summer dress
I lost myself in the city that actually sleeps.
Was it an accident? I took the wrong bus
for the second time this week and,
both times, found myself
at wide, open crossroads,
waiting for the green.

In this city that sleeps, plastic light:
neon signs, crabs and
indecipherable characters
cast a glow on
the damp concrete.
Dripping city, cracked tiles, slow business.
Half-eaten Chinese food, half-smoked cigarette butts,
turning the corners of winding alleyways,
tucked away tables,

a sign of women for sale,
shadowed,
a man fixing the AC
head in the vents.

In this dress, navigation,
Google maps,
brisk walking, night breezes, headphones in,
rogue taxis cutting through air,
red lights, lonely romances.

Seated on the bus, I covered myself in the city's music,
gazed at the fleeting, transient reflection to my right —
me, the street, me, the cars, me, the lights,
to my left, a golfer, a helper, a traveller,
priority sears and artificial shadows of trees,
everyone, earphones in.

Through the haze of the glass,
I blinked: neon hues. Blues, pinks, whites
      — it's me.

The sliding doors folded shut.
I think I'm home.

Home has Arrived

the wind blew into my face
inhale, she says,
it somehow smells like home
i wonder if the air took home with her
and lent it to me
to live a moment in the past
at home, miles away,
but i've rooted here — here's my home now.
the wind has no smell.

Ways of Seeing

I.

I flooded the plank of wood
with paint,
A shade that shadowed my sight,
one that I leaned into
for too long,
so long that it went unseen:
its colour stopped being
a colour, now
a blank, a nothing, a white,
Because the eyes were numb
to the hum of its breath,
now gone,
Now, hands enter — let
them enter this view,
They seem warmer, pinker,
more alive,

I look away, the room,
I look back,
The paint's pistachio-green.

II.

I dreamt of someone last night,
she pierced through
my sleep
as if she knew me,
she said,
'I always watch, so I can see.'
The ceiling cut into view.
'6:38' — I wrote down what
she said
as her
words
became

nothings,

blanks,

whites.

III.

I watched you lean in,
our lips saw each other
for the first
time;
Somewhere else,
someone else shares a kiss,
writes a poem,
hears rain begin,
hears bullets fire, hitches a
ride,
says farewell,

leaves home,
realises home,
tears a book in two,
feels time run out —
I watched you lean out,
I looked away,
and turned back
with sight.

Arrowhead

have I told you that your arrow's made of words?
listen — the architecture of
your language
your syntax,
you shot — straight through
my empty
my abyss, my chest
is about to burst — just, space.

I can fight till my tongue bleeds,
but I swallowed my soul,
and licked the blood
from your lips.

Let Her Dream

there are dreams
where you're not flying,
but floating
till the ceiling
stops you,
where you
push your way out
of the garden
of eden,
to wander.

i must kiss your
tired eyes now,
for fear you'll never
change, and
end up in
the town of
broken dreams,

where ghosts
swallow glass.

the truth is,
you need a new
wave, april tides,
waters that bring about
an eternal spring
where everything
is growing.

Growing Pains

what if to grow

      might mean to first

           sink.

          like bare feet that

              bleed grapes,

   like the

      flooding, of the seed —

how

    you eat the

         air
        around my head

           how

            open wounds

                                                bud new skin, like

                                                new wine,

the skin around the hip   stretches   &   stretches,

                till marks — all veins & rivers — pull
                                through your rubber,

the pain behind your knee,
                calve,

    you grow   out of the things you once loved on your body:
                                        those shoes & skirts.

& you begin growing
                into things, things strange & alien
                & the smell of clean laundry,

                      somehow,

                fitting your mother's blood-stained dress
                        she wore when she first met

                                        your

                        father.

out of his reach
        you grow

                        into the arms of new
                        faces
                        & places,

        but growth marks time
                how time marks flesh,

                        flower-press & fungus
                        in the fold of
                        chapter two,

pencil
on
doorframe.

        growing pains.

        yet, you hang,

        as the gardens of
            babylon do,

            & stretch   &   stretch,

        & finally touch the
        floor.

so, they ask,
    what do you want to be
    when you grow up?

        but the growing,

        reaching,
            expanding,
                unbinding,
            unlearning,
        unfurling,

            has weathered the heart,
            or, perhaps, stretched it.

& a laugh cracks from your teeth
because despite the hurt,
you just don't think
you'll ever
                stop

                        growing.

the angriest people are the radical optimists.

hope buds anger,
bruises my eye till the sky
saw night
the world's your oyster
they say,
they say, you're young
the future awaits.
i know,

hope buds anger
buds bitterness
i know, i bit into a summer plum
in the sweet summer air,
all i tasted was paint.

i know, the world's quite grotesque
and the sun's quite blinding

— it pains me.
hope lies, hope
tries, hope
tried. i know,
i'll lie.

Perspective

We move,
We fall,
We make mistakes,
But regret seethes and simmers
Paradigm shifts
Comes to you like night comes to day
I have the weight of the planets in my chest,
I move,
I fall,
I breathe on.

Why I Write

tuesdays stay grey,
but i braid the day
by writing a poem.

in the braid,
i stay.

Fragments of a Notebook

verbatim,
i rewrite.

(the following are real and unedited clippings from my notebook.)

~

achievements,

average,

<u>week of july 11, 2021,</u>
reflection —
what resonated?

<u>week of july 18, 2021,</u>
reflection —
observations

i want to be like that

    what's the problem in the world?

    marie-kondo-ing life

<u>*scribbles*</u>
    let her dream
    to sleep
    femininity / masculinity

    I am wasting ink by writing this

beyond utility

    women
    self

<u>*notes on beauty*</u>
    pseudo-art
    l'art pour l'art

we should go to the movies alone

plant an idea

no, but really, do people actually see me as a whale?

*'there is no abstract nature that
one is destined to fill'*

the bittersweet,

contact, metal
contact, metal, cream, tongue

is the building on fire?
one day
this loophole
the pillar

i want to reach out and touch things
and feel things touching me back

why am I not excited about ANYTHING???

hangout 13:00
church 17:00

podcast?

I WANT SOMEONE TO WRITE ME A LOVE LETTER.
— it happened

<u>*growth*</u>
       pain

why am I so attached?!
       MOVE ON

if only i could erase people from my life.

Layers of beauty:

                scent — unseen layer
the place was no longer a place

        what if I stopped seeing?

        I THINK I POURED MY LIFE HERE.

              ~

Lined Notebook

to do the undone,
& say the unsaid,
hear the unheard,
& see the unseen

to do, say, hear, see
between the lines

~~here, between the lines,~~
~~is where i want to be.~~

An Ode to Going to the Cinema Alone

to bask under motion picture,
the light of dreams,
crawling for that beam of sun
on a winter's afternoon,
on a sanded oak floor.

i'm warmed by the light of
movies,
alone in the cinema once
again,
where lights fade and
i fade into
forgetting the world, myself,
it's not loneliness,
but healing,

move before me:
twenty-four frames a second,

cut to black — still, twenty-
four. though the screen is still,
the projector
still rolls
a hummingbird's still
yet beats its wings
twenty-four times
a second

a sea of strangers
watch the sam e
story, zoo eyes,
and walk out of the
black box
slightly altered,
slightly renewed.

Park by the Sea

the park grew sad,
my grandma agrees
says it's run dry,
though by the sea

We Went Fishing

the ocean seemed to have
dried up in grains
of salt
salt air, salt hair,
sea salt on
sunlit skin.
on skin, salt wind,
there's something about feeling
the whipping wind on your
skin, in your
face, hair
    (it's called freedom)

so, the shrimp swims
in the wind
as i am on the edge
of everything,
on the angler's boat

bait knocks the seabed,
i stayed ten hours on this boat.
then, what of a lifetime?

i pray that there are enough fish in the
sea for everyone,
for the fishermen fight
and quarrel, and exchange
glances with hidden meanings,
perhaps, the language of
the ocean.

bow,
the anchor, the floor.
this industrial landscape, starboard,
as we traverse the sea,
transposing form,
transposing time,
playing with destiny.

the universe expands.
exponentially.

be the beauty at nothing's beginning,
be the start of your own start
the end to your end,
empty's basin,
baseless,
you're an eye in a body
of eyes, but
a world in a world
of worlds so —
be the nothing, know the nothing
the ebbing, the beautiful nothing the
nothing that binds us the nothing
that beckons us to breathe
breathe breathe
breathe the expanding, the fluctuating, the
growing universe,

be the speck, the breathing, beating,
beautiful nothing
the nothing
that bleeds
bleeds
bleeds,
bleeds —
yes,
bleeds

Acknowledgements

My deepest thanks to these individuals, for without you, this book would not have come into shape, form, or existence. Without you, *Vignette* would have just been another idea in the head of a poet:

Kent Gustavson, my publisher, for your unwavering belief in young people and the power of poetry.

Mohseena Hussain, for your beaming passion in supporting the creation of *Vignette*.

Devi Sahny, for this idea.

Tyshea Holden, my English teacher, for (rather accidentally) introducing me to the names of great poets who I now, at least try to, stand on the shoulders of.

Julicia Lek, for helping me find confidence in my work upon publishing the third issue of 'Lituresque.'

Nicole Kim, Giselle Tang, Chantel Yeo, Ruby Sim, Shilo Ying, Isabel Lee, and Glorianne Ho, for listening to my story, for bringing me out of my rut, for believing in me. Your hearts were what gave me the momentum to write.

Atlas Nagaria, my cousin, for your literary geek-outs and pointing out the fact that I spelt 'eucalyptus' with a 'k.' I've never had so much fun talking to someone about words.

Jack Sykes, for making me write my first poem. Since then, I have not stopped.

Shayna Tjiputra, for giving me space to be vulnerable. You listened to the first poems I wrote without judgement. You encouraged me to write on.

Rei Constance Suherman, my little sister, for being *you*. Though you made it clear that you didn't enjoy poetry, you still heard the words I wrote and mused with me on sleepless nights. I endlessly look up to you.

Mom, for letting me trip and fall, for pulling me up, for never letting me go.

About the Author

Solaia Suherman, born in the spring of 2006, calls the magnetic city of Jakarta, Indonesia her home. She went through a phase in her childhood where every night before bed, she would stick her head in a great book of a thousand poems, reading out, trying to understand each one. Though she can't quite remember anything from it now, this, rather unsurprisingly, began her relationship with poetry.

Today, she finds special joys in cities at dusk, going to the cinema alone, art galleries, eclectic websites, handwritten letters, and oxford commas. As a storyteller who works with both pen and lens, *Vignette* marks her first exploration into poetry – at its heart, her love letter to the world. In fact, it felt only a few dreams ago that, with no sense of proper grammar, she had stapled blank sheets of printer paper together, scribbled in her wildest imaginations, and labelled the flimsy-looking thing, 'my book: wrote by solaia.'

www.ingramcontent.com/pod-product-compliance
Lightning Source LLC
Chambersburg PA
CBHW050930240426
43671CB00020B/2973